Exploring
The Burren

George Cunningham

Series Editor: Michael Ryan

Country House, Dublin

Published in 1998 by
Town House and Country House
Trinity House
Charleston Road
Ranelagh, Dublin 6
Ireland
www.townhouse.ie
Reprinted 2004

In memory of my mother, Margaret Cunningham (1908-1998)

British Library in Publication Data: A catalogue record for this book is available from the British Library.

ISBN 0-946172-59-5

Acknowledgements
The author would like to acknowledge the pioneering work of T J Westropp and the recent research of the late Tom Coffey and of those listed in the bibliography.

He would also like to thank Carmel and Brian Cunningham, Dr David Drew, Dr John Feehan, Michael Greene, Mary Hawkes-Greene and Brian Redmond for their assistance.

The author and publishers thank the following for permission to use their photographs: Burren College of Art (photo 3, pls 7, 8, 10, 12, 13); Dr David Drew (pl 3); Dúchas – The Heritage Service (photo 6); National Museum of Ireland (photo 8, pl 22); Brian Redmond (photos 1, 2, 4, 9, pl 14). All other photographs are by the author.

Cover photograph by Liam Blake
Typeset by Typeform, Dublin
Printed in China for Compass Press Ltd

CONTENTS

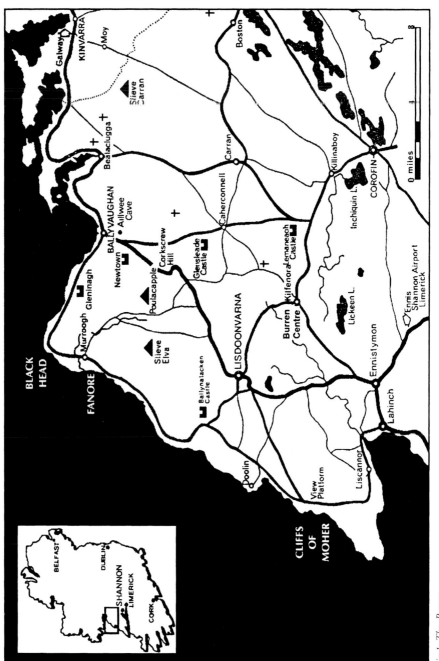

Fig 1: The Burren

INTRODUCING THE BURREN

The Burren (from the Irish *boireann*, meaning a rock or a stony place), lying for the most part in north Clare but also stretching into south Galway, captivates all its visitors. Whatever your interests you will find something special among these fruitful yet bare limestone pavements. Here, terraced hills appear like giant helter-skelters on the horizon together with hectare after hectare of horizontal and fluted stone slabs with vertical fissures, creating an almost lunar landscape.

It would be helpful if one could box the Burren and so give the region definite boundaries: then we could all agree on its area, its population and its monuments. As it is, the Burren is delineated only by one's perception of what it is, and to the botanist that is limestone country. However, that definition would exclude areas commonly considered part of the Burren: the shale-covered Slieve Elva and much of the southern district including the Cliffs of Moher, and towns like Lisdoonvarna, Ennistymon, Lahinch and Liscannor; on the other hand it includes areas sometimes not thought of as part of the Burren – the limestone east lowlands of Gort, the Aran islands and the mini-Burrens around Kilcolgan and Ballinderreen in south Galway.

For most people, the Burren is that area bounded on the north and west by the waters of Galway Bay and the Atlantic, on the south by a line eastwards from Lahinch to Corofin, and on the east by a line southwards from Kinvarra to Kilmacduagh and the freshwater wetlands of east Clare. Geologically speaking, Burren outliers include the Aran islands and the area around Coole Park near Gort in Co Galway. Taking a historical view, we could even include Dysert O'Dea to the south, which, with its monastic and secular settlements, has affinity with the early medieval period of the Burren. The area of the Burren uplands extends over 360 square kilometres with at least another 200 square kilometres covering a variety of landforms.

Photo 1: The southwestern coast of the Burren is dominated by the Cliffs of Moher, seen here with Hag's Head in the distance. These Clare shales or sandstones are over 213m high and lie on top of the older limestone. Rocks like these once covered the entire Burren, but today there are extensive shale remains only at Slieve Elva.

THE CULTURAL LANDSCAPE

Fig. 2: The Burren at the end of the seventeenth century as depicted in Petty's map

6

This is no barren land: successive generations over thousands of years have left indelible marks here for us all to enjoy. Megalithic tombs and ringforts, churches, crosses and castles are found in great profusion in this once well-settled land.

Prehistory

Pollen analysis of the sediment on lake floors near Kilnaboy, at Loch Dá Éan (just west of Mullaghmore) and at the Carran *polje* has revealed much of the vegetation history of the Burren since the last Ice Age. The picture that emerges is of a landscape totally different from the bare limestone that we see today. These muddy 'manuscripts' of pollen reveal that extensive Burren forests of mixed deciduous, pine and yew woodland covered the uplands between 8000 and 7000 BC.

Archaeology

Archaeologists have not found campsites of mesolithic peoples, but it is likely that small hunter–gatherer groups were here from that time on. On present evidence, settlers have definitely been in the Burren over the past 6000 years, clearing and profoundly altering the landscape, probably by overgrazing and burning. By Early Christian times, if not before, the exposed karstland as we know it today had become the dominant feature.

The Burren is one of the most intact archaeological landscapes of Europe, and as the extraordinarily high number of field monuments testifies, this was attractive country to prehistoric people. The Burren is not just a place where stone abounds, it is a world made of stone: stone walls and enclosures, ruined houses of all types and ages, churches, castles and other monuments, a continuous record of settlement. The most ubiquitous monuments are the stone walls, the field boundaries demarcating a 'palimpsest' of enclosures, breathtaking in their abundance and complexity, recording the endeavour of human activity and toil.

Megalithic tombs

The Burren has over seventy examples of the main megalithic tomb-types: court, portal and wedge tombs. The two *court* tombs — Teergonean, on the coast near Doolin, and inland at Ballyganner North, near Noughawal — probably date to after 3800 BC. The excavated *portal* tomb of Poulnabrone had the remains of a maximum of 22 adults and six juveniles. Radiocarbon dating indicates that the burials occurred between 3800 and 3200 BC, up to 1000 years older than was previously understood for that type.

But it is the *wedge* tombs that dominate the late neolithic and early Bronze Age landscape of the Burren. Wedge tombs generally have a wedge-shaped ground plan, with their widest part facing the setting sun, and sloping and tapering east to the rear, though some of those in the Burren look rather box-like and are unusual in having double kerbing. Wedge tombs dominate Parknabinnia, Gleninsheen, Berneens, Poulaphuca and other townlands.

Tentatively dated to 2300–2000 BC (but used well into the Bronze Age), these cemeteries point to extensive settlement, probably by pastoral farming groups attracted here by the year-round grazing. Indeed the tradition of the seasonal moving of cattle is still practised in reverse here, as it has been for millennia: Burren farmers move their cattle to the uplands to winter outdoors, for the 'dry lie' as it is known as locally. As in prehistoric times, the pasture-rich grykes and the calcium-enhanced vegetation ensure that Burren cattle are strong and healthy and consequently very much in demand.

The Bronze Age (*c.* 2200 BC to *c.* 500 BC)

Over 300 *fulachta fiadh* — horse-shoe shaped mounds of burnt stone, built around stone or timber water troughs, the remains of giant Bronze Age cooking-pits — survive in the Burren. The excavated *fulacht fiadh* at Fahee South, near Carran, has been dated to the mid-Bronze Age period.

Recently, some stone circles, ritual sites of the Bronze Age, have been discovered, adding to the emerging jigsaw of knowledge, and there is no doubt that more will be discovered in the Burren. Burial cairns pimple the

Photo 2: Geologically speaking, the Aran Islands are an extension of the Burren. Inisheer (Inis Thoir), the smallest of the three islands, is only a twenty-minute journey by ferry from Doolin.

tops of some Burren hills. A reassessment of the cairn at Poulawack, excavated in 1934, indicated cist burials of only sixteen people over a thousand-year period, from about 3000 BC, truly, like Poulnabrone, a place for the special dead. Prehistoric artefacts from the Burren include bronze daggers, spearheads and the late Bronze Age gold gorget found at Gleninsheen.

The Iron Age (500 BC to AD 500)
There are few datable Iron Age finds in the Burren, and only earthen ring-barrows, such as those near Doolin and Ballinalacken, mark Iron Age burial places. Impressive forts like Caherballykinvarga, near Kilfenora, or Turlough Hill may prove to be older than the Iron Age. Enigmatic Caherballykinvarga, with its *chevaux-de-frise*, may well have been one of the political and economic centres of the leading tribal family of the Iron Age, the Corcu Modruad.

Early Christian period (AD 500–1200)
When Christianity came to the Burren is uncertain, but by the eighth century, the territory of the Corcu Modruad tribe had shrunk to the region of the modern baronies of Burren and Corcomroe and some parts of Inchiquin, and in the twelfth century, this was defined in ecclesiastical terms *9*

Photo 3: The limestone pavements present an array of sculpted delights, fascinating in their enldess variety and providing micro-habitats for the diverse flora (see also pls 6 and 8).

10

as the diocese of Kilfenora, comprising thirteen civil parishes. In any case, the 450 or so cahers, those fortified houses of the well-to-do farmers, point to a relatively large population during the first millennium AD.

One of the most impressive of these cahers is the triple-ramparted, semi-circular, clifftop site at Cahercommaun, deep in central Burren. It was excavated in 1934 by O'Neill Hencken, who concluded that the caher had been used as a cattle ranch in the ninth century. Recent reassessment of the archaeological evidence also shows large-scale weaving activities, suggesting one of the largest wool-processing stations in early Ireland. Indeed, sheep shelters of indeterminable age are found on the limestone, and the Burren hills have continued to be recognised as ideal sheep country into modern times. In recent times, there were only half as many sheep as cattle, but sheep numbers are growing again — which is not good news for the flora.

Churches

The legacy of a millennium and a half of Christian worship remains very tangible as a story in stone in the Burren. There are up to eighty-two ecclesiastical sites in the Burren, covering a millennium of worship. As well as church ruins, cemeteries, hermitages and monastic enclosures we have holy wells (deemed to be efficacious in the relief of various ailments), saints' seats or 'beds', and penitential stations, all rooted in a distant past.

Kilfenora, Kilmacduagh, Oughtmama, Templecronan, Killinaboy and Dysert O'Dea are early church places of national importance. Kilmacduagh's origins are to be found at St Colman's hermitage, Keelhilla, under the magical Slievecarran. Colman's fame led to the foundation of Kilmacduagh, the monastery named after him (Colman was the son of Duagh); its churches and leaning round tower still dominate the eastern approaches to the Burren.

Kilfenora, 'the city of the crosses', is still a vibrant settlement. Its cathedral still serves the community, even though its chancel is now roofless. Not so Oughtmama which, with its large enclosure, three churches, blessed well, stream and horizontal mill, in a very fertile though depopulated valley, must have been at the centre of all activity towards the end of the first millennium. Nearer to Carran, Templecronan is just as isolated today. But again its exquisite twelfth-century masonry and decoration, cross fragments and

11

saints' 'beds' point to medieval activity of which we now know nothing.

Killinaboy and, further south, Dysert O'Dea all have suites of buildings and features of varying medieval importance: churches, round towers, crosses, Hiberno-Romanesque decoration, even a sheela-na-gig (a carving of a naked female, posed to emphasise the genitalia).

Medieval times (AD 1200–1700)

The Anglo-Norman incursions into Ireland had little known impact on life in the Burren. O'Loughlin and O'Connor chieftains, descendants of the Corcu Modruad, continued to control their patrimony under the lordship of O'Brien of Thomond (an area covering the northern part of the province of Munster). The Cistercians arrived late in the twelfth century and, following an endowment by Donal Mór Ó Briain, King of Thomond, they built an abbey at Corcomroe, *Sancta Maria de Petra Fertili* (St Mary of the Fertile Rock). Substantial ruins with special features and much decoration survive in the valley at the foot of Corker Pass, along a major route between Connacht and north Munster.

The principal southern approach to the Burren remains the Corofin to Killinaboy route, just as it was in medieval times when the Cromwellian General Ludlow made his much-quoted remarks at Leamaneh about the

Photo 4: With Doonagore restored towerhouse in the background, this Iron Age ring-barrow (cemetery mound) is one of several that survive in the Doolin area. Others are found near the road to Lisdoonvarna from Ballinalackan Castle.

12

Photo 5:
Bishopsquarter lies to
the north of
Ballyvaughan
village, near
Drumcreehy
medieval church.
The sand dune
system here, although
relatively minor in
comparison to
Fanore, is important.
Across the water from
the beach lies the
Martello Tower at
Finavarra, still
awaiting the never-
to-be Napoleonic
invasion from
France.

place: 'not water enough to drown a man, wood enough to hang one, nor earth enough to bury him'. Thomas Dineley, the Londoner who tried to journey through here in the 1680s, had to record, 'only one narrow road here and no side road'.

Medieval remains

The record in stone is much more revealing than the manuscript record, particularly from the fifteenth century onwards. Parish churches were built; towerhouses, the minor castles of the Gaelic lords, became the norm. Some cahers continued in use or were re-used; others were fortified with gateways. One such, Cahermacnaghten, the location of a celebrated Brehon law school of the O'Davorens, continued to be occupied until the collapse of the Gaelic way of life at the beginning of the seventeenth century.

Dispersed or small-cluster settlement seems to have been the pattern in medieval times. Kilfenora and Noughawal with its market stone-measure, both rooted in monasticism, are among the only surviving villages to pre-date the eighteenth century. Gleninagh with its towerhouse, holy well (important enough to be 'housed' in the sixteenth century), big house and church, lost out to more sheltered Ballyvaughan. By the early 1800s this

13

village, also an O'Louglin medieval stronghold, had become the economic and administrative centre for the southern shores of Galway Bay; similar shifts happened to the settlements at Newtown/Rathborney, south of Ballyvaughan, and to Muckinish, north of the village.

If we include all the towerhouses of the local ruling families of the time, such as the O'Loughlins, the O'Connors, the O'Heynes and the O'Shaughnessys, and Brehon lawyers like the MacClancys, we have incomparable examples of almost every building form and feature. Cylindrical, rectangular, L-shaped towers contain murder holes, machicolations, batters, spiral stairs, stone vaulting, decorated fireplaces, mullioned windows and state-of-the-medieval-art garderobes. Other than these architectural details there is almost a total absence of dating evidence.

Thankfully, some towers like Doonagore, Newtown, Dunguaire, Dysert and Ballyportry have new lives. Gleninagh, Ballinalackan, Fiddaun, Shanmuckinish, Gregans have responded to some care, lately or in the past, though others like Glensleade, Castletown, Liscannor and Muckinishnoe deteriorate daily — a remarkable heritage crumbling. Máire Rua's glorious fortified mansion of strong tower and seventeenth century house at Leamaneh unfortunately remains off limits to visitors.

Photo 6: One of the most unusual of the hundreds of Burren cahers (stone forts) is to be found at Ballykinvarga on the southern boundary zone. Defended by a chevaux de frise, its circular enclosure measures 50m in diameter. This is an impressive structure by any standards, possibly reflecting the prestigious stature of its owner.

Photo 7: The ruins of one of three early Christian churches surviving at Oughtmama. Three St Colmans are associated with the place. St Colman's well, believed to cure eye complaints, is still visited and votive offerings are always present.

Photo 8: This late Bronze Age socketed and looped axehead (c. 800–400 BC) was found at Oughtmama. Considering that the Burren was extensively settled in prehistoric times, as we can tell from the wedge tombs and other earthworks found in the area, finds of artefacts are surprisingly rare.

Photo 9: When stone ceases to be a readily available material, earthen ringforts become the norm. This single-bank example of a rath is located at Tullagh, a little over 2km east-south-east of Kilfenora.

NATURAL HISTORY OF THE BURREN

Landform and geology

However you draw your personal Burren boundaries, this is a complex and diverse landscape of limestone pavements, terraced hills and closed valleys, wetlands, grassland, woodland, scrubland and a varied coastline. It is the finest example of karstic (limestone-covered with underground drainage) landscape in Ireland. The limestone was laid down at the end of the Lower Carboniferous period over aeons of time, probably beginning some 325 million years ago. It varies in texture and contains fossils of sea-lilies, molluscs and coral-like creatures. Massively bedded and over 800 metres thick, the limestone of the west and north Burren lies on Galway granite, which dies away to the south-east and so allowed earth movements to form hills like Mullaghmore and Knockanes.

Later, in the Upper Carboniferous period (about 280 million years ago), younger rocks of shale and sandstone were laid down, covering and protecting

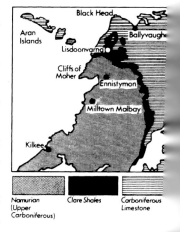

Fig. 3 Simple geological map of west Cl

16

(continued on p. 33)

Pl 1: Mullaghmore, with its gentle folds, lies on the eastern edge of the Burren. To the west, the terraced hills appear more stable, as they lie on a bed of granite. Because of plans for an interpretive centre near its base, Mullaghmore has become an icon for conservati nists.

Pl 2: Erratics, rocks stranded by the retreating glaciers, are found everywhere in the Burren. This is Cloch Scoilte *on the western coast.*

17

*Pl 3: The Fergus
River sinking
underground near
Kilfenora. The dry
valley beyond shows
the former course of
the river.*

Pl 4: The polje *at
Carran was
originally a closed
depression. Deepened
by glaciation, it
became the largest
Burren turlough.
Pollen analysis of its
deposits has indicated
extensive forest cover
here in postglacial
times*

18

Pl 5a: Coole Lough, made famous by Yeats and other literary figures in Lady Gregory's circle, is one of the many turloughs or winter lakes of the eastern Burren. In summer the water recedes to that of a small lake, but layers of a papery surface and black moss on the vegetation indicate former water levels.

Pl 5b: Following Lady Gregory's death in 1932, Coole House fell into disrepair and, despite protests and pleas, was eventually demolished in 1941. Only the outline of the house's foundations now marks what was once a welcoming retreat where great men 'came like swallwos and like swallows went' (WB Yeats, 'Coole House' 1929).

19

Pl 6: Limestone pavements at Poulsallagh. The lines of weakness in the rock eventually become the fissures or grykes. The slabs of limestone are called clints.

Pl 7: For many visitors, the Burren orchids are a special delight, but thankfully orchid mania is almost a thing of the past, and today's orchids are allowed to grow in their own habitat. They really will not flourish elsewhere. May to July is the best time to see them in abundance. This is the pyramidal orchid (Anacamptis pyramidalis).

20

Pl 8: Many of the Burren flowers find shelter in the grykes of the limestone pavements.

Pl 9: The mountain avens (Dryas octopetala) *grows in association with the spring gentian, but is more widely distributed throughout the region. Indeed, it is difficult to avoid walking on clusters of them in many areas.*

Pl 10: The spring gentian (Gentiana verna) *flowers in abundance in the Burren in early summer, particularly during May. Used extensively as the symbol of the Burren, it is as common as daisies in some fields.*

Pl 11: During the summer in the Burren, geraniums do well, particularly the striking magenta bloody cranesbill (Geranium sanguineum). *Its name derives from the long reddish fruits that it bears.*

21

Pl 12: The pearl-bordered fritillary (Boloria euphrosyne) is a woodland butterfly of Europe. In Ireland it is found only in the Burren.

Pl 13: Herds of feral or wild goats still roam the Burren uplands. They perform a good service in keeping the scrubland, particularly the strongly growing hazel, in check.

Pl 14: Acre-sized Crab Island lies just off the coast of Doolin; the ruin is that of a coastguard hut.

Pl 15: Lake Muree (or Muirí), near the tip of Finavarra peninsula beneath Burren Hill, extends over 14 hectares of salt water, which teems with bird life. University College Galway's marine research station is nearby.

23

Pl 16: The Burren teems with relics of past settlement, some of the recent past, others thousands of years old. This forgotten road is at Bleak Head.

Pl 17: The very fine example of a fulacht fiadh (cooking place) at Murrough, near Fanore. The horse-shoe-shaped mound is composed of the discarded burnt stones used to heat the water.

24

*Pl 18: Stone walls of
every type are found
in the Burren. Some
are thousands of
years old, and others
were erected in recent
times. But in what
way they relate to the
other settlement
features or tombs
found on the
landscape remains
enigmatic and
debatable.*

*Pl 19: This typical Burren upland
landscape shows a 'palimpsest' of
settlement. Only a detailed survey of
every field and wall coupled to research
excavation will reveal their place in the
settlement picture of the Burren.*

25

Pl 20: Poulnabrone portal tomb was described by its excavator, the archaeolgist Ann Lynch, as 'a place for the special dead'. Her excavation in the 1980s, which dated the use of the tomb or cemetery to between 3800 and 3200 BC, showed that it was used for fewer than 30 burials. The remains were mostly a jumble of disarticulated bones deposited some time after death in Poulnabrone. Artefacts found in the burial chamber included a bone pendant, a polished stone axe, pins and scrapers.

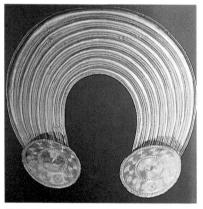

Pl 21: The wedge tombs of the Burren point to significant settlement at the end of the Stone Age and into Bronze Age times. Although they seem to differ in construction, they all adhere to a wedge-shaped ground plan. This wedge tomb at Gleninsheen lies near to where the late Bronze Age gorget was found.

Pl 22: The Gleninsheen gold gorget or collar was found in the early 1930s by a local farmer, Patrick Nolan, and is one of eight such collars surviving from about 800 BC. Two terminal discs are attached to a crescent of sheet gold, all highly decorated. The collar may be seen in the National Museum of Ireland.

26

Pl 23: One of the oldest megalithic tombs of the Burren is the court tomb found at Teergonean. The forecourt or open area of the tomb (presumably where mourners gathered) is highlighted in the illustration.

Pl 24: A wedge tomb at Creevagh, which was inhabited during the nineteenth century.

27

Pl 25 a and b: Towerhouses were erected as the strongholds of the Irish chieftains from late in the fifteenth century. Two O'Loughlin fortifications were at Seanmuckinish (a) and Gleninagh (b), both on the shores of Ballyvaughan Bay. What remains of Muckinish and its bawn were preserved during the nineteenth century. Gleninagh's fabric was conserved by the state in the recent past.

28

Pl 26: The early stone cross at Noughawal is one of the indications that the parish medieval church had its origins in early Christian times. However, it is salutary to remember that stone, particularly when it has no decoration, is almost impossible to date accurately.

Pl 27: Granted lands in the eastern Burren, St Colman mac Duagh, built his extensive monastery, Kimacduagh, on the edge of the Burren Today, its ruins include Ireland's only leaning round tower.

Pl 28: One of the finest Burren vistas unfolds from the road at Corker pass above Corcomroe. With Aughinish in the foreground, the coastline of Galway may be glimpsed across the bay. The ruins of Kinturley tidal corn mill, in the left centre of the picture, lie near the western weir of Corranroe Bay. The fast-flowing tide into and out of the shallow inlets was harnessed to provide power for the mill.

Pl 29: One of the loveliest of the small early churches of the Burren is to be found at Templecronan. Its original lintelled doorway hints at an earlier date than the twelfth century. One of the two stone reliquaries or church-shaped tombs is stated locally to mark the burial place of St Cronan.

30

Pl 30: Newly restored Newtown rises from its pyramidal defensive base to a cylindrical towerhouse of probably sixteenth-century origin. Once the stronghold of the O'Loughlin clan, today it tells their story and that of the Brehon law and the Bardic schools of the Burren. The 1300m nature trail at Newtown is one of the most informative on the diverse ecology of the Burren.

31

Pl 31: Traditional crafts are once again finding outlets in the Burren, and the hazel wood at Aillwee Cave is being coppiced for a variety of uses, both practical and decorative.

Pl 32: Intensive farming practices in the Burren are leading to much reclamation of the limestone pavement into grassland. Recent reclamation work resulted in these modern 'tumuli' between Kilcroney and Caherconnell.

32

cont. from p 16

the limestone (they still do on the Cliffs of Moher and in the southern areas of the Burren) until the glaciers of the past two million years moulded the hills, carved the valleys and stranded both granite and limestone erratics on the pavements. Terracing on the hills occurred when the vertical joints in the limestone weathered and large blocks tumbled off.

The same vertical joints became fissures or *grykes* on the pavements, forming horizontal slabs known as *clints*. As the limestone continues to dissolve, the clints become rounded and *fluting* occurs. Each pavement becomes a miniature landscape carved with hollows, pits and channels caused by the action of water on the limestone.

Underground

With over 60 per cent of the Burren uplands showing exposed rock, it is easy to think that stone defines its essence, but one soon learns that water is everything here: it gave birth to the region, it gives it life and ultimately it will be its agent of destruction. But, paradoxically, even with over 1500mm of annual rainfall (as compared with 700mm in the east of Ireland), there are only one or two surface streams; at 4km long, the Caher, flowing into the sea at Fanore, is the most permanent. As is usual in karstland, drainage is underground.

To date over 50km of underground caves — the active river systems of the area — have been charted in the Burren and the exploration is by no means complete. There is an 11km branched system of underground caves under Slieve Elva. The awesome swallow-holes of this system are at Poulelva and Poulnagollum, and its forty smaller sink-holes or potholes (locally called *sluggas*) dot Elva's eastern flank. Slieve Elva is covered with shale, which is impermeable to water, but on the eastern side of the mountain, the shale meets limestone. What happens is that the water flows along the shale until it reaches the limestone, which, being porous, allows the water to seep underground. This means that most of the known active systems have their sink-holes on this geological boundary.

The underground cave of Poll an Ionain near Ballinalackan has a 7m-high stalactite, one of the most dramatic in Europe. The Doolin system, entered from a 12m pothole at Fisherstreet, has submerged sea caves with marine flora

Photos 10: The roofless chancel of Kilfenora is alive with interesting medieval detail.

10a: The mitred head of a bishop dominates this fifteenth-century traceried wall tomb on the north side of the chancel.

10b: This rather stiff episcopal tomb effigy was probably carved some time after the Black Death (1348–9).

34

and fauna of exceptional interest. But these are all active systems and can only be explored by experienced speleologists, and then only with great caution. For most visitors, the fossil cave at Aillwee, Ballyvaughan, provides safe glimpses of this underworld.

Glen of Clab, north of Carran, is a good example of a collapsed underground cave in the upland reaches of the Burren. Sandstone boulders, remnants of its shale cover, remain strewn about the valley floor, and Pollavan at the head of the valley is the relict of its swallow-hole. The decay of another cave resulted in the conical pits and ravine near the pass of Mám Chatha, south-east of Ballyvaughan, and other cave collapses created the hundred or so closed depressions or valleys, which form part of the High Burren. The largest of these, at Carran, being over 3km long, is technically known as a *polje*.

Turloughs

Unique to Ireland, the turlough (in Irish *turlach*) is very much a feature of the east Burren wetlands. Turloughs are winter lakes, hollows that fill or empty as the water-table fluctuates. A turlough can cover as much as 150 hectares or more. A distinctive algal papery substance and the blackish moss *Cinclidotus fontinaloides* on the vegetation indicate the level of flooding.

Flora

For over a century and a half the Burren's main claim to international fame has been its diverse and enigmatically contrasting flora. Here on the limestone pavements, growing side by side at both sea level and on the uplands are arctic, alpine and Mediterranean species. The arctic and alpine plants, the highlights of which are the spring gentian (*Gentiana verna*) and the mountain avens (*Dryas octopetala*), are the residue of late glacial tundra vegetation. As the climate in Ireland became warmer, Mediterranean species, such as the delicate maidenhair fern (*Adiantum capillus-vernis*) and the dense-flowered orchid (*Neotinea maculata*), took hold and flourished.

Not so easy to explain is the survival and cohabitation of lime-lovers and lime-haters here on the western fringes of Europe. Plants with a preference for acid soil,

10c: The cathedral's three-light east window is separated by triangular pillars with carved capitals of clerics.

10d: Kilfenora once had seven crosses — hence its name 'city of the crosses'. The west cross, or 'cross in the fields', dates from the twelfth century. It is thought to have had a shrine at its base attached to the cross shaft.

35

such as ling (*Calluna vulgaris*), will be found growing wherever a thin layer of peat has built up over the limestone.

Plants whose normal habitat is upland country happily grow at sea level in the Burren; and plants normally found in woodlands thrive on the open treeless limestone. Mild winters with a noticeable absence of frost, varying soil types, microclimates, the warm limestone and the shelter of the grykes are all probable factors in their continued survival here.

Late spring and early summer in the Burren provide the most dazzling display of colour. Often it is the abundant colourful clusters of native flowers that catch the eye: yellow mats of bird's foot trefoil mingling with mounds of purple thyme; or the fields of primroses and cowslips, particularly along the Caher river valley — the Burren remains one of their Irish strongholds. But the special Burren plants are spectacular: gentians make intense blue carpets; differing slightly after 8000 years of separation from their European counterparts, they are also individual plants of elegance and beauty, 'bluer than anything else which grows'. The large-flowered butterwort (*Pinguicula grandiflora*) is another firm favourite. The dryas too, with their creamy petals and woody stems, are in full bloom at this time. Later in the summer, the sheer profusion of the magenta bloody cranesbill (*Geranium sanguineum*) leaves indelible memories on the landscape of the mind.

Orchids dazzle too, all twenty-two species of them: treasures such as the early purple, bee, fragrant, fly, frog and that Mediterranean speciality, the dense-flowered orchid, whose survival here is still puzzling botanists. In 1980, the doyenne of Burren scholars, Maryangela Keane, re-found the greater butterfly orchid (*Platanthera chlorantha*) near Mullaghmore; it had been collected in Ballyvaughan in 1912, but botanists had remained unconvinced of its presence here.

The sheltered habitats of the grykes are full of surprises. Here you will find the exquisite burnet rose (*Rosa pimpinellifolia*) and many of the twenty-four species of Burren fern, including hart's tongue (*Phyllitis scolopendrium*), red fern (*Ceterach officinarum*) and the maidenhair from the Mediterranean, with its shining black leaf-stems and pale green leaflets, all providing year-round interest.

36

Fauna

Only two of the thirty or so species of butterflies and moths found in Ireland are not found in the Burren. This indicates a healthy environmental balance. One moth, the Burren green (*Calamia tridens o.*), discovered as recently as 1949, is unique to the region. Ballyryan and the neighbouring Oughtdara are butterfly- and moth-rich and seem also to be the home-base of one of the largest feral goat herds that roam the uplands of the Burren. The wooded hollows provide habitats for badgers, foxes, stoats and pine martens (*Martes martes*), and a wide variety of nesting and perching birds. All seven Irish species of bats are found, often hibernating in souterrains.

Although it has its highlights, the Burren is not in general a bird habitat of note. The eastern lakes have colonies of wildfowl, waders, gulls and wild swans, 'Their headstrong looking heads, tucked or cresting or busy underwater' (Seamus Heaney). Redshanks, common sandpipers and mallard can be found breeding around the turloughs.

The inner reaches of Ballyvaughan and Galway Bay provide important winterage for Brent geese and long-tailed ducks, and, dramatically sited at the Burren's wouth-west edge, the Cliffs of Moher have been described as a summer seabird city of guillemots, puffins, kittiwakes, gulls and fulmars.

The Burren's Atlantic shoreline is tempered by warm waters coming from southern oceans. It offers contrasting land- and seascapes from the spectacular Cliffs of Moher in the south to the long-fingered shallow inlets of Aughinish and Finavarra in the inner reaches of Galway Bay. Sandwiched along the seaboard are the terraced cliffs at Doolin and Black Head; the beaches and dunes at Fanore and Bishopsquarter; the saltmarshes of Rine; marine-rich islets like Illaunloo with its seals and Deer Island with its 300 nests of cormorants; and the ecologically significant areas of Poll Salach and the Flaggy Shore.

Purple sea-urchins, oyster beds in the shallow bays — Red Bank oysters are still famous — and diverse communities of marine life are to be found in the submerged caves. Unfortunately, much of this underworld is only accessible to divers, but the limestone terracing that steps into the sea does offer glimpses of its treasures. The brown seaweeds are of interest, particularly those on Carrig Fhada reef at the Flaggy Shore. At the field station there,

Photo 11: The Cistercian abbey of Corcomroe rises unexpectedly among the 'fertile rocks' at the foot of Abbey Hill. We can only guess at what the landscape was like when those pioneering monks arrived there at the beginning of the thirteenth century.

Professor Máirín de Valera of UCG has added considerably to our knowledge of the Burren's seaweed flora. Mackerel, pollack, dogfish and conger are among the fish that anglers catch from the rocks. Bass and flatfish may be caught from the golden sands that cover the reefs of black limestone at Fanore.

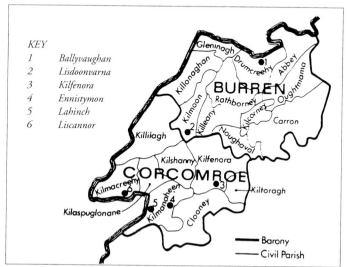

KEY
1   Ballyvaughan
2   Lisdoonvarna
3   Kilfenora
4   Ennistymon
5   Lahinch
6   Liscannor

38

Photo 12: Some cahers were fortified in medieval times with strong gateways, almost like miniature towerhouses. Cahermore, above the Ballyvaughan valley, with its lintelled doorway, is one such example.

THE BURREN TODAY

Agriculture and tourism

The Burren has always been an agricultural landscape of extensive farming practices, but today's intensive farming poses enormous threats not only to its ecosystems and ecological diversity but to the karstland's very survival. Man has always been a 'rearranger of stones', but it takes a modern bulldozer only a day to rearrange destructively a landscape that has uniquely evolved and survived for over 15,000 years, and is now in itself a prime asset. Research suggests that the area of limestone has been halved since famine times (1840s), and that four per cent of the pavements have been converted to thin grassland or upland roads since the early 1970s.

Photo 13: Additional proof that some cahers were inhabited down to late medieval times is provided by the settlement and law school at Cahermacnaghten, between Noughawal and Corkscrew Hill. Here Brehon lawyers, the O'Davorens, carried on a celebrated school until English rule in the seventeenth century finally ended such Gaelic traditions.

The population of the Burren fell from 4000 to 2500 between the beginning of this century and 1991, but there is now cause for optimism with vibrancy in every community. With a balanced strategy, combining public and private interests, these communities can provide the leadership to safeguard the Burren, not only for their own future generations, but for the countless thousands who are privileged to visit each year.

However, marrying mass tourism to a fragile landscape will always pose problems. The Cliffs of Moher has in excess of half a million visitors each year, and Aillwee cave attracts more than 100,000 annually. Today's visitors want to do a little more than take the waters at the spa at Lisdoonvarna and see the flowers. By any standards, this intoxicating landscape on Europe's western edge should be a world heritage site, but we do not have even a cursory listing of all its monuments, let alone a comprehensive knowledge, wall by ancient wall, field by prehistoric field, of this strange country. Awareness of its uniqueness would certainly be a start.

The Burren inspires

40

The Burren has always inspired talent: writers, poets, artists, musicians and craftspeople have all come under its spell. Early in the twentieth century, at the water's edge at Coole, Thoor Ballylee, Mount Vernon and Doorus, Lady Gregory and WB Yeats played pivotal roles in promoting the Irish literary and theatrical world, 'working to add dignity to Ireland'. With Coole House (at Gort, in Co Galway) long demolished, it really is a journey of the mind to retrace the footsteps of its visitors, a Who's Who of Irish literary giants: O'Casey, Shaw, Synge, AE among others. The initials of many famous people, including those of Shaw (GBS) can still be seen on a large copper beech in the gardens at Coole.

Betjeman's 'Stony seaboard, far and foreign/Stony hills poured over space' became an anthem for Burrenites, while Heaney's 'Aisling' and 'Postscript' evoke differing landscapes. Michael Longley's prayer-poem 'Protect the Burren, Our Lady of the Fertile Rock' grew out of a recent controversy about the building of an interpretive centre at Mullaghmore, a sad wrangle that has divided local people and has been a terrible waste of money and energy.

Many artists are now living in the region, and distinctive craft forms are slowly emerging, inspired by the shale and the limestone. From strongholds at Doolin and Kilfenora, Irish music and dance have never been as traditionally inventive, and 'I've been to Doolin' has become an international catch-phrase.

We the privileged ones, the armchair readers of the Burren's landscape and those of us who share its magic, have a debt to pay: please care for this wondrous country.

Photo 14: Leamaneh Castle, an O'Brien stronghold, still stands as a southern gateway to the Burren. The original fortification (pictured here on the right) was a late-fifteenth-century towerhouse. To this structure a fortified house, with large mullioned and transomed windows was added, probably as a result of the marriage of Máire Rua MacMahon, one of the Burren's most famous women, to Conor O'Brien in 1639. The story of Máire Rua and her efforts to recapture the estates for her children make stirring reading.

41

INTERPRETING THE BURREN

Useless to think you'll park and capture it
More thoroughly...
(from 'Postscript' by Seamus Heaney, in *The Spirit Level* 1996)

It is a journey of a lifetime to capture this multi-faceted landscape. However, even a short visit is memorable and there are many centres where you can find information to make your visit even more rewarding, listed here in alphabetical order.

Aillwee Cave
Guided circular tours into the showcave of the Burren underworld, south-east of Ballyvaughan. Aillwee's access building has won many awards, not least for its environmental softness. In the adjoining hazel scrub a resident woodsman reveals many traditional practices: coppiced woodlands and charcoal production, wattle hurdles and related crafts.

The Burren Centre
Situated in Kilfenora, the historic and ecclesiastical capital of the Burren, this centre provides a good general introduction to the region. Guided tours of the adjoining cathedral and its renowned high crosses are available.

The Burren Way
Signposted walk over the western terrain of the Burren. With accompanying text, it brings you actively through many thousands of years of Irish history, highlighting some and allowing the visitor to discover others on a magical landscape.

The Burren Xposure
Large-screen audiovisual presentations (using black and white slides, with colour for the flora) of all aspects of the Burren: geology and landscape; archaeology, history and traditions; flora and fauna. Adjoins the superbly sited Whitethorn craftshop and restaurant at the water's edge just north of Ballyvaughan.

Cliffs of Moher and O'Brien's Tower

Visitor centre at Ireland's and indeed Europe's highest vertical cliffs, rising to over 213m and stretching for almost 8km. O'Brien's Tower, at the highest point, was constructed in the nineteenth century as a viewing platform.

Coole Park, Kiltartan Cross and Thoor Ballylee

Three visitor centres exploring the literary associations of the Gregorys, WB Yeats and other figures of the Irish Literary Revival. Guided walks and interpretation of the natural history of the turloughs and woodlands at Coole.

Corofin Heritage Centre

Major genealogical research centre for Co Clare in former parish church of the Church of Ireland community; Tau Cross and other Burren artefacts on display.

Dunguaire Castle

Restored medieval towerhouse at Kinvara on the northern seashore of the Burren; medieval banquets held during the summer months.

Dysert O'Dea Archaeology Centre

At a restored towerhouse on the southern approaches to the Burren; archaeological walks to St Tola's early monastery with its twelfth-century ruins, and to other sites in the vicinity.

The Liscannor Stone Story

This begins at the Rock Shop in Liscannor village, where a video outlines the history of shale or flag quarrying in the area. Quarrying continues at Lough Doolin, a short distance inland on the shale hills. Here, under one roof, in a hands-on experience, all the various textured rocks may be seen while the flags are lifted, cut and dressed for small or large contracts.

Newtown Castle and Nature Trail

Restored cylindrical towerhouse of the O'Loughlins just south of Ballyvaughan, now part of the Burren College of Art; information and displays on the Brehon law and bardic schools of the Burren; adjoining guided nature trail of 1.3km to the terraced foothills of Cappanawalla mountain.

43

Spa Wells Centre

On the shale at the edge of the limestone lies Lisdoonvarna's famous Victorian spa complex and health centre. Its therapeutic mineral waters of sulphur, iron and magnesium have been dispensed since the eighteenth century.

Photo 15: By 1917, WB Yeats had purchased the ruined towerhouse at Ballylee for £35. When restored, he rechristened it his 'thoor' (from the Irish túr meaning 'tower') and spent many summers there. His volume of poems The Tower *was inspired by Thoor Ballylee.*

44

SELECT BIBLIOGRAPHY

Brady Shipman Martin, *Burren National Park Draft Management Plan*,
    February 1996
Cunningham, George, *Burren Journey*, Limerick, Shannon Development: 1978
_____, *Burren Journey West*, Limerick: Shannon Development, 1980
_____, *Burren Journey North*, Ballyvaughan:
    Burren Research Press, 1992
_____, *The Burren Way*, Shannon: Shannon Development, 1991
D'Arcy, Gordon and Hayward, John, *The Natural History of the Burren*,
    London: Immel, 1992
Drew, David, 'The Burren, Co Clare' in FHA Aalen, Kevin Whelan and
    Matthew Stout (eds), *Atlas of the Rural Irish Landscape*, Cork:
    Cork University Press, 1997
Feehan, John and O'Donovan, Grace, *The Magic of Coole*, Dublin:
    OPW, 1993
Gibbons, M and Condit, T 'Recent research and developments in the Burren'
    in *The Other Clare*, vol 13, 1989. All volumes of *The Other Clare* are
    essential reading for serious study of the area.
Keane, Maryangela, *The Burren*, Dublin: Easons, 1980
Nelson, E Charles and Walsh, Wendy, *The Burren - a companion to the wildlife
    of an Irish limestone wilderness*, Kilkenny: Boetius Presss, 1992
O'Connell, JW and Korff, A (eds), *The Book of the Burren*, Kinvara:
    Tír Eolas, 1991
O'Connell, Michael (ed.), *Burren, Co. Clare*, IQUA Field Guide No. 18, 1994
O'Connell, Michael and Jelicic, Ljubica, 'History of vegetation and landuse
    from 3200 BP to the present in the north-west Burren, a karstic region of
    western Ireland' in *Vegetation History and Archaeobotany 1*, 1992,
    pp 119–40
Robinson, TD, 'The Burren Uplands' in *The Book of the Irish Countryside*,
    Belfast: Blackstaff Press, 1987, pp 80–5
_____, *The Burren: A Map of the Uplands of North-West Clare*,
    Galway, 1977
Rynne, Etienne, 'The Early Iron Age in County Clare' in *North Munster
    Antiquarian Journal*, vol xxiv, 1982, pp4–18
Sheehan, John, 'The Early Historic Church-sites of North Clare' in
    North Munster Antiquarian Journal, vol xxiv, 1982, pp29–47
Spellissy, Sean and O'Brien, John, *Clare: County of Contrast*, 1987
Swinfen, Averil, *Forgotten Stones*, Dublin: Lilliput, 1992

GLOSSARY

Brehon law
A native Irish legal system that pre-dated English rule and held sway in parts of Ireland up to the seventeenth century

caher
Ringfort made of stone, elsewhere known as *rath, lios, dún, caiseal,* depending to some extent on the building material used

chevaux-de-frise
Defensive feature, made of upright stones, originally designed to halt horsemen

clints
Horizontal slabs of limestone

erratic
A large rock carried by glacial action; erratics are usually different from the rock types in the surrounding landscape

fluting
Channels cut into rock by action of water

garderobes
Latrines in towerhouses or castles; the term comes from the practice of storing clothes near latrines for preservation

granite
A hard, igneous rock

grykes
Fissures in limestone pavements

igneous rocks
Rocks formed by volcanic action or solidification of magma; 95% of rocks are igneous

karstic landscape/karstland
Rough limestone country with underground drainage, named after the Karst district east of the Adriatic

limestone
A sedimentary rock, very prevalent in the Burren, which is porous and so is easily permeated by water

limestone pavement
A landscape of flat slabs of limestone, characteristic of the Burren

machicolation
Protruding turret on medieval building from which missiles were dropped on attackers

mesolithic
Period between early stone age *(palaeolithic)* and late stone age *(neolithic)* times, after the last Ice Age and before the beginning of agriculture

46

polje

A sizable closed valley or depression originally caused by cavern collapse and enlarged by solution and erosion

pollen analysis

A process that allows the botanical history of an area to be inferred from the pollen-grains found in the various layers of its soil; pollen-grains survive for long periods of time and can be identified after thousands of years, thus giving a picture of the type of vegetation that was in the area at various points in its history

sandstone

A sedimentary rock of consolidated sand

sedimentary rocks

Rocks formed by the compacting of sand, mud or silt. They are younger than igneous rocks and constitute only 5% of rocks on earth

shale

A non-porous rock that splits easily into flags (Moher shale or flags are widely used in the Burren for flooring and decorative purposes)

swallow-hole/sink-hole

Hole in the ground into which a stream disappears, forming an entrance to a cave or cave system

slugga

Local term for sink-hole or swallow-hole

speleologists

People who explore and study caves

turlough

From the Irish *turlach*, a winter lake; it disappears in summer, when the water-table falls